P9-DCV-033

Ronda Rousey

By Jon M. Fishman

AMAZING ATHLETES

Lerner Publications ◆ Minneapolis

Lerner Publications Company
A division of Lerner Publishing Group, Inc.
241 First Avenue North
Minneapolis, MN 55401 USA

For reading levels and more information, look up this title at www.lernerbooks.com.

Library of Congress Cataloging-in-Publication Data

Names: Fishman, Jon M.
Title: Ronda Rousey / by Jon M. Fishman.
Description: Minneapolis : Lerner Publications, [2016] | 2017. | Series: Amazing Athletes | Includes
     bibliographical references, webography and index.
Identifiers: LCCN 2015050919 (print) | LCCN 2015051343 (ebook) | ISBN 9781512413335 (lb : alk. paper)
     | ISBN 9781512413670 (pb : alk. paper) | ISBN 9781512413687 (eb pdf)
Subjects: LCSH: Rousey, Ronda—Juvenile literature. | Women martial artists—United States—
     Biography—Juvenile literature.
Classification: LCC GV1113.R69 F57 2016 (print) | LCC GV1113.R69 (ebook) | DDC 796.812092—dc23

LC record available at http://lccn.loc.gov/2015050919

Manufactured in the United States of America
1-39791-21328-3/4/2016

TABLE OF CONTENTS

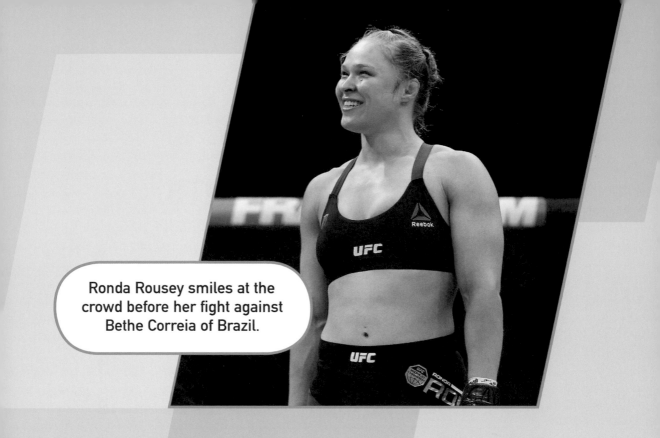

Ronda Rousey smiles at the crowd before her fight against Bethe Correia of Brazil.

FAST AND FURIOUS

On August 1, 2015, **mixed martial arts (MMA)** fans gathered in Rio de Janeiro, Brazil, for a huge fight. Champion Ronda Rousey faced Brazilian Bethe Correia. Lights blinked and cameras flashed in the arena. The crowd hummed with excitement.

Correia had the benefit of fighting in her home country. But most MMA fans expected Ronda to win. She had never lost an MMA match. Her **armbar** move had taken down fighter after fighter. Most people couldn't last even one minute against her.

Ronda and Correia tangle in the first few seconds of their match.

Ronda and Correia face off in the arena.

Yet Correia wasn't impressed with Ronda's record. The Brazilian had said unkind things about Ronda before the fight. At the **weigh-in**, Correia yelled in Ronda's face, but the champion stayed calm and focused.

The night of the fight, the buzz in the arena grew as Ronda entered the **octagon**. As soon as the match began, she moved toward Correia. Instead of trying for an armbar, Ronda swung her fists. Correia ducked and moved back.

About 20 seconds into the fight, Ronda pushed her opponent. Correia fell back and rolled to the edge of the octagon. Ronda moved in and let loose a flurry of punches as Correia got to her feet. Ronda's left fist landed on Correia's jaw. The Brazilian stumbled. Seconds later, Ronda landed another big punch. Correia tipped over and fell to the mat. The **referee** stopped the fight. Ronda had won again!

Ronda's win against Correia took just 34 seconds. Four of Ronda's earlier **professional** wins had taken even less time.

Fans around the world cheered her 12th win in a row. Stars such as NFL quarterback Aaron Rodgers posted messages about Ronda on Twitter. "It is REALLY fun watching someone who is THAT dominant," Rodgers wrote.

Ronda forgave the unkind things Correia had said. "I consider the matter settled," Ronda said after the fight. As MMA's biggest superstar, she would rather focus on her bright future.

Ronda wears her championship belt after the fight.

Ronda *(right)* and her mother, AnnMaria *(left)*, attend the UFC on Fox event at the Staples Center in Los Angeles in 2012.

LITTLE FIGHTER

Ronda Jean Rousey was born on February 1, 1987. She lived with her father, Ron, in Devils Lake, North Dakota. AnnMaria, Ronda's mother, lived 120 miles away because of her job in Minot, North Dakota. Ronda's older sisters, Maria and Jennifer, lived with AnnMaria. Their half sister, Julia, was born later on.

Doctors wanted Ronda to live alone with her father. She didn't grow and learn as quickly as her sisters had. It took her a long time to begin walking, and she had trouble speaking. Doctors thought Ronda and her father should spend time together to work on her speech without distractions.

Ronda grew up in rural North Dakota.

By the time Ronda was six years old, she could speak full sentences. The time alone with her father had paid off. It had also made Ron and Ronda close. She loved her father very much and bragged about him to her friends.

Around this time, Ron hurt his back in a sledding accident. He flew in a helicopter to a hospital for surgery. But his back didn't get better due to a rare blood disorder that kept him from healing. He was in pain and spent a lot of time at the hospital. Eventually, doctors told Ron that he probably wouldn't live much longer. When Ronda was eight years old, her father took his own life.

When Ronda learned to swim, Ron could see that his daughter was a good athlete. "You're going to win the Olympics," he told her.

Ronda was shocked and upset. The most important person in her life was gone. AnnMaria decided the family needed a new start. Ronda moved with her mother and sisters to Southern California.

Ronda's half sister, Julia *(left)*, and mother, AnnMaria *(right)*, attend a match between Ronda and Cat Zingano at the Staples Center in 2015.

In California, Ronda made a surprising discovery. She found her mother's old scrapbook. Inside were photos of AnnMaria competing in **judo**. In 1984, AnnMaria had won a gold medal at the World Judo Championships. She was the first person from the United States to become a judo world champion. The images stunned Ronda. She had never thought of her mother as a fighter.

"NO STOPPING HER"

Ronda was in deep mourning for her father. To find something positive to focus on, she took up judo with her mother's help. Ronda was sure she would like the sport. She had spent a lot of time play-wrestling with her sisters. "We used to fight every single day," Ronda said.

Judo training tested Ronda's toughness. When she was 12 years old, she broke one of her toes during practice. Her mother made her run laps anyway. With tears in her eyes, Ronda limped as she ran. She felt sorry for herself, but she learned an important lesson that day. "Even if you're hurt, you can overcome it and fight," she said.

These kids train in a judo lesson.

Ronda showed promise on the judo mat. As a teenager, she worked hard and gained muscle. "Once she started, there was no stopping her," AnnMaria said. Ronda decided she wanted to try out for the 2004 Olympic Games. To reach her goal, she began spending time in Boston to train with judo coach Jimmy Pedro.

Jimmy Pedro is a judo world champion and two-time Olympic medalist.

Pedro helped Ronda master the finer points of the sport. Judo athletes are called **judokas**. They win matches by scoring more points than their opponents. Points are given for small **throws** and **holds**. Judokas can also win matches by scoring an **ippon**. This happens when a judoka throws an opponent and slams her to the mat. An ippon can also be reached by strong holds that force a judoka to submit.

Ronda's best hold was the armbar. She held an opponent to the mat. Then she hooked her legs around the other judoka's body and grabbed her arm.

Ronda learned the armbar from her mother. AnnMaria had ended many judo matches with the hold.

Ronda pulled on the arm while squeezing with her legs. Most judokas submitted quickly.

If they didn't, their arm could be injured. The threat of injury didn't stop Ronda from using the armbar whenever she could. "I'm taking the same risks [other judokas] are," she said.

Ronda's famous armbar has taken down many opponents.

Ronda *(left)* competes against Grace Jividen for the chance to go to the 2004 Olympics.

BRONZE JUDOKA

In June 2004, Ronda tried out for the Olympics. To make the United States judo team, she had to beat Grace Jividen. Jividen was almost 40 years old. Judo fans expected the **veteran** judoka to easily beat 17-year-old Ronda.

Ronda reacts to winning her match against Grace Jividen.

Jividen and Ronda fought a close match. Both judokas huffed and puffed. Jividen lunged and tried to throw Ronda. But the younger fighter was too fast and strong. She threw Jividen to the mat for an ippon. Ronda won the match and made the United States team! "I'm really just in shock," she said. "It will take a while to sink in."

Ronda was the youngest judoka at the 2004 Olympic Games in Athens, Greece. She didn't earn a medal, but making the team proved that she could fight with the top judokas in the world. Over the next few years, Ronda continued her judo training. By 2008, she was the top female judoka in the United States.

Ronda was ready to earn an Olympic medal. At the 2008 Olympic Games in Beijing, China, she lost to Edith Bosch. But Ronda would still take home a bronze medal if she beat Annett Boehm of Germany. Boehm was tall and strong, but she couldn't take Ronda down. Ronda won the bronze medal!

In 2008, Ronda became the first woman from the United States to ever win an Olympic medal in judo.

Ronda took home the bronze medal in the 2008 Olympics.

After the Olympics, Ronda thought about her future. She felt ready to step away from judo. But other than a new car and a surfboard, she wasn't sure what she wanted. Ronda knew people involved with MMA. Unlike judo, MMA rules allow punching. "I might learn how to throw a punch," Ronda said. "But I'm not making any promises."

During the next year, Ronda tried to create a life away from sports. She thought she could use a break for a while. But without something to train for, she felt unhappy. She also missed the thrill of winning a fight. Ronda began training to become an MMA fighter.

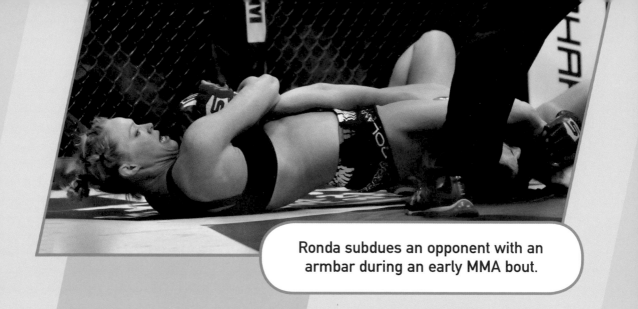

Ronda subdues an opponent with an armbar during an early MMA bout.

ACTION STAR

In 2010, Ronda fought her first MMA **bout**. It was an **amateur** fight against Hayden Munoz. As the match began, Ronda circled to the left. Suddenly she dove and pulled Munoz to the mat. Munoz twisted and punched. But Ronda stayed on top. She wrapped her legs around Munoz. Ronda grabbed Munoz's arm and pulled. Munoz submitted, and just like that the fight was done. It had lasted only 23 seconds!

"I felt like I was in a movie," Ronda said after beating Munoz. "I never had a whole room of people cheering for me." It was a feeling that Ronda would get used to in the years to come.

Ronda shows off her UFC bantamweight championship belt in 2012.

On March 27, 2011, Ronda fought her first professional MMA match. She beat Ediane Gomes with an armbar after 25 seconds. She won each of her next three matches in less than one minute. Then Ronda took down four more opponents. She won each of her first eight professional bouts with an armbar!

Ronda had become a huge star. She was the most popular fighter in MMA. She appeared on TV commercials and talk shows. In 2014, she played a character named Luna in the movie *The Expendables* 3. She later had additional action roles in the *Furious 7* and *Entourage* movies. Ronda said that acting made her "super nervous," but she soon relaxed and had fun.

Ronda's best friend is her big white dog, Mochi. She is a type of dog called an Argentine mastiff.

She won three more fights before beating Bethe Correia in August 2015. Ronda had a perfect record of 12–0. On November 14, 2015, she fought Holly Holm in Melbourne, Australia. Holm's strong punches kept Ronda away. In the second round, Holm kicked Ronda in the face. Ronda fell to the mat, and the referee stopped the fight. She had lost her first MMA match.

Ronda lost a bout for the first time in her career to Holly Holm *(left)* in 2015.

Ronda took time off to heal after the loss. She was sore and sad. But she knows that reaching for her dreams is a risk worth taking. "I always say you have to be willing to get your heart broken," she said a few weeks after the fight. Ronda will continue to chase her dreams in the octagon and on the movie screen.

Ronda remains a strong fighter with an impressive record.

Selected Career Highlights

2015 Lost to Holly Holm for her first MMA defeat
Defeated Bethe Correia in 34 seconds
Defeated Cat Zingano in 14 seconds

2014 Defeated Alexis Davis in 16 seconds
Defeated Sara McMann in 1 minute, 6
seconds

2013 Defeated Miesha Tate in 10 minutes, 58
seconds
Defeated Liz Carmouche in 4 minutes, 49 seconds

2012 Defeated Sarah Kaufman in 54 seconds
Defeated Miesha Tate in 4 minutes, 27 seconds

2011 Defeated Julia Budd in 39 seconds
Defeated Sarah D'Alelio in 25 seconds
Defeated Charmaine Tweet in 49 seconds
Defeated Ediane Gomes in 25 seconds in Ronda's first professional
MMA match

2010 Defeated Hayden Munoz in 23 seconds in Ronda's first amateur
MMA match

2008 Won a bronze medal at the Olympic Games

2004 Competed as the youngest judoka at the Olympic Games

Glossary

amateur: something done for fun or experience

armbar: a hold that bends the arm painfully

bout: an MMA or boxing match

holds: moves that keep a fighter from moving

ippon: a winning point in judo

judo: a fighting sport that awards points for throws and holds

judokas: judo athletes

mixed martial arts (MMA): a fighting sport that allows kicks, punches, and wrestling

octagon: the eight-sided ring where MMA matches are held

professional: something done as a job for money

referee: a person who makes sure fighters follow the rules during an MMA match

throws: moves that cause a fighter to fall to the mat

veteran: someone who has been doing something for a long time

weigh-in: an event before an MMA match where the fighters are weighed

Further Reading & Websites

Fishman, Jon M. *Manny Pacquiao*. Minneapolis: Lerner Publications, 2016.

Savage, Jeff. *Aaron Rodgers*. Minneapolis: Lerner Publications, 2012.

Wells, Garrison. *Brazilian Jiujitsu: Ground-Fighting Combat*. Minneapolis: Lerner Publications, 2012.

The Official Website of the Ultimate Fighting Championship
http://www.ufc.com
Visit this site to view MMA schedules, videos, and much more.

Sports Illustrated Kids
http://www.sikids.com
The *Sports Illustrated Kids* website covers all sports, including MMA.

USA Judo
http://www.teamusa.org/usa-judo
This website is full of information about the United States judo team.

Expand learning beyond the printed book. Download free, complementary educational resources for this book from our website, www.lernereSource.com.

Index

Photo Acknowledgments

The images in this book are used with the permission of: © Matthew Stockman/Getty Images, p. 4; Ricardo Moraes/Reuters/Newscom, p. 5; Celso Pupo/Zuma Press/Newscom, pp. 6, 8; AP Photo/Mat Sayles/Invision, p. 9; © America/Alamy, p. 10; © Harry How/Getty Images, p. 12; © Stephen Dunn/ Getty Images, p. 14; © Ute Grabowsky/photothek images UG/Alamy, p. 15; © Matthew Stockman/Getty Images, p. 16; © Stephen Dunn/Getty Images, pp. 18, 19, 20; © Nelson Ching/Bloomberg/Getty Images, p. 22; © David Dermer/Diamond Images/Getty Images, p. 24; AP Photo/The Canadian Press/Neil Davidson, p. 25; © Paul Crock/AFP/Getty Images, p. 27; AP Photo/ Jae C. Hong, p. 28; AP Photo/Mark J. Terrill, p. 29.

Front cover: AP Photo/Jae C. Hong.

Main body text set in Caecilia LT Std 55 Roman 16/28.
Typeface provided by Adobe Systems.